Guide to Bonus and Incentive Plans

Duncan Brown

Towers Perrin

BUILDING RELATIONSHIPS ■ PRODUCING RESULTS™

The Chartered Institute of Personnel and Development is the leading publisher of books and reports for personnel and training professionals, students, and all those concerned with the effective management and development of people at work. For full details of all our titles, please contact the Publishing Department:

Tel: 020 8263 3387
Fax: 020 8263 3850

E-mail: publish@cipd.co.uk

The catalogue of all CIPD titles can be viewed on the CIPD website:
www.cipd.co.uk/publications

Guide to Bonus and Incentive Plans

Duncan Brown

First published 2002
Reprinted 2002

Cover design by Curve
Designed and typeset by Beacon GDT
Printed in Great Britain by Short Run Press

British Library Cataloguing in Publication Data
A catalogue record for this book is available from the British Library

ISBN 0 85292 955 2

Chartered Institute of Personnel and Development,
CIPD House, Camp Road, London SW19 4UX

Tel: 020 8971 9000
Fax: 020 8263 3333
Website: www.cipd.co.uk

Incorporated by Royal Charter. Registered charity no. 1079797.

Contents

Introduction

Throughout my working life I have always been in some type of bonus scheme. Starting off as a 'green' personnel graduate trainee at Vauxhall's plant in Luton, my pay slip used to have £17 every week labelled as a 'productivity bonus'. As I walked through the plant each morning, watching the cars on their inexorable progress down the production track, I often used to wonder how it worked. But nobody else seemed to understand the complex formula, and it only ever varied by a few pence from week to week anyway.

Manufacturing industry, the traditional heartland of employee bonus schemes, continues to decline in the UK, and the last car will shortly roll off the production line at Luton. Yet as I, like many, have moved into service- and knowledge-based sectors, the applications of these pay schemes have continued to expand. The financial services and information and technology sectors display the highest levels of coverage, with the bulk of employees in fast-growing employment areas such as call centres now covered by them. I'm not sure my current consultancy bonus affects my behaviour much more than the Vauxhall scheme did, but at least I have a few personal objectives, and it certainly has a greater impact on my discretionary spending, ('No Tabitha, you can't have a new bike until next April!').

As I document in the first chapter of this guide, discussions about bonuses and all forms of performance pay seem to be invariably shrouded in extremist and over-simplistic views, hype and controversy, which prevents a rational consideration of the topic. In my 20 years of employment we appear to have somersaulted in the UK from limited usage and general disdain and hostility ('incentives, ugh, that's what salespeople have!'), to the current situation of expansion – and the adulation of Chancellors and chief executives.

Indeed, I seriously worry that the recent history of individual performance-related base pay is in danger of being repeated with bonus and incentive schemes: excessive hype and exaggerated claims, followed by rapid expansion and copy-cat introductions, leading inevitably to failure to live up to the huge expectations, ending up in disillusionment and rejection.

In the past year I have worked on a number of briefs to introduce, for example, a team incentive where we have ended up concluding that the situation is simply not appropriate for it. I suspect that many other employers have been making a less detailed assessment and a more Pavlovian response. This is undoubtedly one of my reasons for writing this guide. It's useful to learn to swim before you dive into the pool, but it's even more important to check there is water in there first!

The reality in the majority of employers today is that most people recognise the reasons that bonus and incentive are becoming more common, and probably grudgingly admit that a well-designed and operated scheme does have some effect on them. Correspondingly, a badly designed and inappropriate scheme definitely has the reverse effect, as this guide will illustrate.

The aim in this short guide is therefore in a hopefully low-key, balanced, realistic and practical manner to do four things for you:

> **Chapter 1:** first to document just what is actually happening in the bonus and incentive field and why;

> **Chapter 2:** then to describe the major types of scheme that we are seeing in the UK today, and features and trends in design;

> **Chapter 3:** moving on to consider the research on their effectiveness and the key overriding considerations that you need to make in determining whether to use them and how to make them work in your own organisation (the assessment of the existence and depth of water in the pool, to continue with my earlier swimming analogy);

> **Chapter 4:** finally to attempt to give you the basics of how to swim, so to speak, with a step-by-step guide to introduction and operation, and reflecting some of the training which we give to our consultants at Towers Perrin.

Terminology

I don't want to get too hung up in complex terminology but there are probably a few important terms to define at the outset. This guide is about bonus and incentive schemes, that is pay plans that offer cash lump sums to employees in relation to some aspect of their individual and/or collective performance. In North America variable pay is perhaps a more common nomenclature.

As I describe in chapter 2, I tend to use 'incentive' to refer to plans with a more specific and direct intent to improve future results and impact individual behaviour, and 'bonuses' as more general schemes to reward and reinforce performance. I am not going to consider performance-related base pay or merit pay plans, share schemes or non-cash recognition schemes, which are all described in other CIPD publications. I am also not covering cash allowances unrelated to performance. Nor, unfortunately, in a short guide do I have space to separately consider incentives for specific employee populations such as executives, direct sales, financial trading or call centre staff.

However, I have tried to include as many practical examples as possible, from my own work and a wide range of organisations, to illustrate the major types and trends. Indeed, if as the geneticists tell us, diversity and mutation is the key to successful evolution, then I think we must regard the current trend towards a much greater variety of schemes, between and inside of organisations, as a very healthy sign.

So while I hope this guide can give you a reasonably quick overview of the main types and issues involved in bonus and incentive scheme usage and design, remember that local tailoring to your own needs and circumstances is perhaps the most critical ingredient for success.

Duncan Brown
Principal, Towers Perrin

◘ **Documents the growth in bonus and incentive plans in the UK**

◘ **Explains the reasons for this growth**

1 | The rise of bonus and incentive pay

The hype

'Globally, bonuses are HOT!' proclaimed an earnest speaker at the recent WorldatWork conference in Nashville. There certainly seems to be widespread admiration and advocacy for them at the moment, with support expressed by politicians such as the UK Chancellor of the Exchequer, the Deputy Taoiseach in Ireland and the European Union's Council of Ministers, and chief executives ranging from Jack Welch at General Electric to Michael O'Leary at Ryanair.

The HR press regularly refers to employers who are introducing or redesigning plans. Employees ranging from Marks and Spencer's shop assistants, to London Underground and Virgin rail workers, HM Customs and Excise staff and the UK's top 3,000 Senior Civil Servants have all experienced new bonus and incentive schemes in recent months. Variable pay plans are increasingly in evidence in the rest of Europe and Asia, be it for production employees at Seiko Epson and BMW, or pharmacy assistants in Russian retailer 36.6.

Of course, there is nothing new in this, and employers have for centuries used cash lump sums to try to motivate their staff to perform. Piecework payments for garment-producing homeworkers pre-dated the Industrial Revolution. Profit-sharing schemes were evident in the nineteenth century in sectors as diverse as French house painting and German farming. Gainsharing plans, which according to a recent Incomes Data Services Study are the fastest-growing type in the UK, were pioneered in the designs of Scanlon and Rucker in the USA in the 1920s and 1930s, and recent reinterpretations of the famous Hawthorne experiments there suggest that the role of group bonuses in achieving higher productivity was seriously underestimated.

But the trend is not totally positive and upwards. Some have used their criticisms of individual performance-related base pay to advocate its replacement by team bonus schemes. For example, the influential Makinson report on performance pay in government has led the five central departments studied to commit to a bonus opportunity for all staff, equivalent to at least 5 per cent of base pay. US experts Schuster and Zingheim have as one of their six universal principles of reward management that results should be rewarded by variable pay.

But other critics, such as Pfeffer and Kohn, attack all forms of monetary incentivisation as exploitative and damaging to intrinsic motivation and to a mutually beneficial employment relationship. Highly geared sales commission plans in sectors such as insurance, pensions and double glazing are being reformed and withdrawn in response to evidence that they work against consumer interests. Piecework schemes are also on a longer-term declining curve, with evidence that they have encouraged output at the expense of quality in industries such as construction. In fact, in the UK the New Earnings Survey suggests that only 15 per cent of the workforce is covered by bonus and incentive plans – a slight decline from the proportion a decade earlier.

So just what is the real picture with bonus and incentives schemes in the UK today?

The growth

A range of recent research studies from the CIPD, Towers Perrin, the CBI, the Industrial Society, and Industrial Relations Services all indicate that the impression of growth in the incidence, coverage and levels of payment within bonus and incentive plans is indeed accurate. To give some examples:

◘ Towers Perrin's study of 150 mostly large private sector, UK-based organisations found that 93 per cent operated bonus and incentive plans, with the majority having three or more different schemes internally; 70 per cent had introduced or reformed plans in the previous three years and 62 per cent had further changes planned, most commonly in the direction of more plans, covering more staff with higher earnings opportunities (see Figure 1).

◘ The Industrial Society's wider study of 1,100 organisations found that 70 per cent operated bonus and incentive schemes of some type.

◘ The latest CBI Employment Trends survey shows that 63 per cent of the 670 participants have individual pay for performance of some type, 48 per cent with profit-sharing and 19 per cent with team pay.

◘ In the CIPD's study, 35 per cent of employers used profit-sharing and 19 per cent team bonus schemes.

◘ The IRS's 2000 trends review found 28 per cent of organisations using individual incentives, 20 per cent profit-sharing, 16 per cent other types of lump sum cash payments, 5 per cent team rewards, and 3 per cent gainsharing.

◘ The Workplace Employee Relations Survey in 1998 found 32 per cent of establishments with profit-related bonuses, and 52 per cent (representing 64 per cent of employees covered by this very large study) with some form of variable pay.

The effects of the introduction and extension of these various types of plan on the nature of people's pay package in the UK can be seen in the Towers Perrin data – see Figure 2. We asked companies to indicate, for three generic levels of staff, the proportion that actual levels of bonus represented in their total take-home pay. Figure 2 demonstrates that senior staff generally have higher bonus levels than lower-paid employees.

This is no surprise, given that incentives have always been more popular for roles – be it salespeople, City traders or board directors – where the individual's impact on results is most obvious and easiest to measure. But the general upward trend in average payments at all levels is marked, and indeed has been one of the reasons given for the somewhat erratic movements in the national average earnings statistics in recent years.

So why, beyond what The Economist termed the 'follow-the-herd' syndrome, are employers making greater use of bonus and incentive plans?

Figure 1 | Forecast changes in bonus and incentive plans over the next three years

Introducing new bonus plans	72%
Increasing levels of variable pay	39%
Introducing/extension of individual performance-related base pay	39%
Increasing plan coverage/membership	29%
Shift in emphasis in performance measures from individual to team	20%
Removal of current bonus plans	12%

Source: Towers Perrin

Figure 2 | The increasing levels of variable pay in the UK

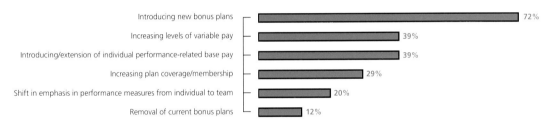

Staff Category	Mix of base pay and variable pay		
	3 years ago	Current	3 years in future
Senior executives	80 : 20	75 : 25	69 : 31
Management/professional staff	88 : 12	84 : 16	79 : 21
Non-management staff	96 : 4	93 : 7	89 : 11

Source: Towers Perrin

The rationale

Perhaps not surprisingly in our increasingly global, intensely competitive and resource-constrained economy, and with people representing up to three-quarters of the total costs and value added by organisations in the services and information sectors, the main reasons given in these studies for using incentives are to improve business performance and strengthen the links between individual performance and corporate results.

> *'...the main reasons given...for using incentives are to improve business performance and strengthen the links between individual performance and corporate results.'*

These were the top goals for over 70 per cent of participants in both the Towers Perrin and Industrial Society research. Thus, at Marks and Spencer, the extension of bonuses to cover all staff is geared towards supporting the company's turnaround and encouraging employees to 'go the extra mile'. Reducing costs, interestingly, was listed by very few companies, and these schemes are invariably being introduced without any reduction in base pay. Only 4 per cent of the organisations in the Towers Perrin study were using them to replace performance-related base pay increases although, as reported by Incomes Data Services, the Portman Building Society has recently returned from merit-based pay to a general pay award, with cash bonuses 'to maximise messages about good individual performance'.

However, another important agenda is evident from the stated aims: a somewhat 'softer' and less direct means of using schemes to improve business understanding and build commitment to the organisation and the achievement of its goals. Twenty-five per cent, for example, were using plans to improve teamwork, 41 per cent to improve employee communications and participation, and 43 per cent to reduce employee turnover. Lawler even defines bonus schemes as, 'pay programmes designed to involve employees in improving performance'. Thus at retailer Dixons, as well as encouraging a stronger focus on customer service, store bonuses have been introduced to involve all staff, not just the salespeople, in improving profitability.

A variety of studies, for example by Sheffield University and David Guest for the CIPD, demonstrate the powerful business impact that creating this type of high-involvement culture can have on business results. We shall consider these in more detail in Chapter 3. The failure of many companies using incentives to address this 'softer' agenda in practice is, as we shall see, a major limitation on their effectiveness. Before considering the effectiveness of schemes however, we need to define and describe the main types of plan referred to above.

◘ **Defines the main types of bonus and incentive plan**

◘ **Describes the characteristics, strengths and weaknesses of each type**

2 | Definitions, types and trends

A classification

Accepting Milkovich and Newman's broad definition of bonus and incentive plans as 'any form of variable pay scheme which rewards employees on the basis of performance' there clearly are different aims, types and features in the myriad of different schemes now evident in the UK employment landscape. They can be classified in respect of the groups of employees covered, such as a factory or sales scheme; or in respect of the performance measures used, as for example in profit sharing or productivity plans.

However, a useful framework that we use to think about them in Towers Perrin is in respect of two variables:

◘ the level in the organisation at which they operate eg company-wide or location-based

◘ the primacy of goals in terms of providing future incentives to perform, or rewarding past performance.

The major types of scheme are illustrated against this framework on Figure 3, and each in turn is briefly described below. The relative incidence of these schemes in the Towers Perrin research was as follows:

◘ profit-sharing: 46 per cent of companies, a slight decline from our previous study

◘ gainsharing: 11 per cent

◘ team-based: 23 per cent – up by 5 per cent in the past three years

◘ individual employee plans: 63 per cent

◘ combination plans, the fastest growing variant: 42 per cent

◘ project and ad hoc bonuses: 28 per cent.

Profit-sharing

Profit sharing schemes generally operate on an annual basis and share out a proportion of corporate profits among all employees on a common basis, normally as a percentage of base pay. During the 1990s they spread rapidly in the UK on account of the favourable tax treatment afforded to government-approved profit-related pay schemes, which at their peak encompassed over 4 million employees.

Since then the coverage has declined somewhat, although many large employers such as Boots and John Lewis simply carried on with their schemes without any favourable tax treatment. Pendleton's research suggests that there are now 2,500 schemes in operation. Legislative encouragement also explains their popularity in the Netherlands (55 per cent of companies), and in France, where they are compulsory for companies with over 50 employees.

The research on these schemes, as for all-employee share schemes, suggests that outside of very small enterprises they do not strongly influence the day-to-day efforts and behaviour of employees. They are not incentives, and this factor – in the wake of increasing competition – has led the major accounting firms to replace their common or service-linked formulae for distributing

profits amongst partners with individual performance-related allocations.

However, there is nonetheless research support for the European Union Council's recommendation that our employers should introduce these schemes. They are associated with favourable employee attitudes and reduced levels of staff turnover. Pendleton found their use was also associated with a basket of other positive HR practices, including employee participation mechanisms and staff development programmes. Indeed, many of the earliest schemes in the UK were introduced in the nineteenth century by philanthropic Quaker employers. And in terms of the business returns of a committed workforce

Figure 3 | A classification of the main types of incentives and bonus schemes

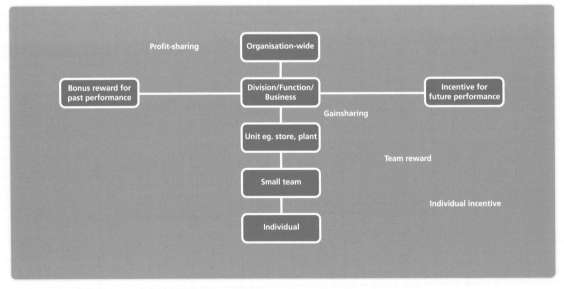

supported in this way, Wallace Bell's study of over 1,000 UK companies found that total investor returns were almost twice as large amongst companies with profit-sharing schemes compared with those without.

An evident trend in the use of all types of bonus and incentive plans at present is the use of a wider variety of performance measures. A number of organisations have modified their profit-sharing plans to include non-financial measures, both to reflect the interests of major stakeholders other than shareholders, and to give employees more direction in terms of how high financial returns are to be achieved. Thus one of the water utilities has replaced its general staff profit share with a scheme incorporating a balanced scorecard of measures. Annual goals are set in respect of financial returns, customer satisfaction, process excellence and staff development, with maximum payments of £500 pa.

However, the lack of direct impact has led other organisations to look at alternative or additional schemes.

Gainsharing

The productivity-driven plan developed by union official Joseph Scanlon and introduced in 1938 at the failing La Pointe steel company, which shared out the resulting cost savings with employees at the plant, made a major contribution to the company's survival. Successful examples can still be seen in what remains of the US steel and heavy

industry today, with Ameristeel achieving significant productivity gains in the 1990s. General Electric, Travellers Insurance, Whirlpool Corporation and Sony Electronics, as well as UK companies such as BP, Blue Circle and British Energy, have followed their example.

> *'A number of organisations have modified their profit-sharing plans to include non-financial measures...'*

Gainsharing plans essentially share with the employees a fixed proportion of the gains beyond an agreed performance target, again generally on an equal basis. They typically operate at a location or site level, and the aim is to have a more direct impact on employees' performance, generally using operational and controllable cost measures. Thus on BP's North Sea oil rigs, a 'cost per barrel of oil produced' target would be set. If the employees on the rig beat that target, by producing more oil at the targeted cost, or the same volume at lower cost, then they would share equally in a fixed proportion of the gains. The results have been generally favourable, in the North Sea, at Grangemouth and in Alaska.

However, as with any scheme, the effectiveness depends on participants relating to the measures employed. A technology company using a scheme in one of its UK plants found that employees individually did not feel able to influence the plant performance measures used. In a pharmaceutical company's plant in Ireland, a scheme was rendered worthless when a corporate sourcing decision to move elements of production to another plant created a major decline in output.

Changes in the manufacturing technology and process can also create problems. A food manufacturer in the south east of England ran a scheme from the 1970s until the mid-1990s. Payment levels rose from 5 per cent to over 20 per cent of base pay, and yet almost all of the productivity improvements driving this originated from the introduction of new technology, and was nothing to do with the efforts of the employees.

Team-based schemes

According to Katz and Kahn, 'organisation practice has been slow to recognise the motivating power that group rewards can provide'. But as Lawler observes, given the prevailing 'trends towards lateral structures, broad roles and employee involvement' and the resulting effort put into improved teamworking, 'team-based pay plans are likely to become much more popular'. Over 40 per cent of organisations in the CIPD research were considering their introduction, although only 5 per cent of the employers in the Towers Perrin research had actually done so in the past three years.

Organisations relating the performance of small groups or teams of employees to performance are typically trying to have a much more direct incentive effect on their behaviour, the strength of their teamwork, and the results they produce. The incentive cycle is typically shorter, with performance measured over a month or over a quarter.

Again, they tend to be most common in 'front-line' areas such as sales and customer service activities, be it in bank and building society branches, retail shops, and customer service centres. As in the first case study profile, a number of firms have introduced them to address the downsides of excessive individual incentivisation.

Thus a European car manufacturer has introduced dealership bonuses covering all of the staff in its sales outlets. These reward total revenue achieved and customer service ratings in each dealership on a quarterly basis. It encourages sales, technical, service and administrative staff to work together in maximising the range of services provided to customers, rather than exclusively rewarding just the salespeople for their personal sales through commission.

Kwikfit similarly shares a fixed proportion of over-budget operating profits with the work team in each outlet. And Boots the Chemist is introducing store-based bonuses, using customer satisfaction measures in its new chain of Pure Beauty stores. According to project head Simon Potts, 'one of the biggest factors limiting growth in this market is the type of women who work behind the counters – many customers are scared of them'.

Team plans have also been used successfully in back office administrative activities and production areas. Thus at Sun Life Assurance each processing team has a cost reduction target. Exceeding this target on a quarterly basis generates a bonus pool, which is then paid out according to the level of customer service performance, measured through mystery shopper assessments, error ratios, and cases handled per hour. Payments are up to 10 per cent of base pay. The scheme has been associated with controllable cost reductions of 30 per cent, and improvements in turnaround times of 45 per cent.

Coventry Building Society had similar success when it replaced a profit share with branch-based incentives in 1998. Improvements in team working and staff understanding of business measures accompanied the associated growth in sales.

With the switch from linear to cell-based organisation in the production of silicon chips, many manufacturers now employ team-based incentives. They have also been used successfully in a number of public sector settings, for example by Coventry and Kent councils and Portsmouth NHS trust, where they often seem to have a better fit with the culture and values than individual incentives.

But if the results are so good, then why isn't the incidence of team incentives growing much more rapidly? Why of the 14 per cent planning their use in IRS's 1998 research did only 2 per cent subsequently introduce them? One factor is undoubtedly the regularity of reorganisations in many companies, which disrupts the definition of teams. In one pharmaceutical research facility we found that staff were generally on more than one project team, and that the membership of teams shifted during the course of each project. A fixed team incentive would have risked introducing damaging rigidities into this creative and flexible

organisation. Central functions such as personnel and finance also tend to be difficult to cover and, in the Towers Perrin research, typically fewer than 25 per cent of total employees in an organisation are included.

Competition between teams can be another potential downside. In an administrative centre of a major insurance company we found that the team incentive had made teams reluctant to take on new and potentially lower-performing staff, or contribute to any site-wide initiatives. There were even rumours that an internal transfer system had developed with monetary inducements for the best individual performers to join a new team!

The demotivating effects on high individual performers, particularly if there is any of what the psychologists refer to as 'free-riding' going on amongst other team members, can be another problem. In the recently opened tele-centre of a major bank we found that despite a stated corporate value of teamwork, which they wanted an incentive to reinforce, with multi-skilled agents able to handle all the needs of each caller then high performance in the centre was primarily dependent on the individual contribution of each agent. The incentive that was introduced was therefore primarily individual, with a small team modifier.

In fact, despite often being praised as a more effective replacement for individual performance pay, most organisations with team incentives also have some form of individual performance pay in place as well. Fewer than 2 per cent of team schemes studied by the then American Compensation Association were not operated alongside individual approaches. Abosch and Reidy's research found that 'companies rated the most successful programmes as having a balance between the two'.

The evidence also suggests that while pay can reinforce the performance of an effective team, it does not turn a bad team into an effective one. Team pay, like all incentives, relies on other supporting initiatives to enable it to contribute to improved performance. One study in the semiconductor industry looked at four variables related to effective teamwork: the layout of the facility, the design of jobs, the feedback of performance information, and the use of team rewards. None on its own produced high performance, but when three or more were employed in the move to cell-based manufacturing then productivity improved significantly.

Abosch and Reidy's conclusion is that 'the best approaches are customised to the situation, to suit the activities of specific teams and ... evolve over time as a team's identity and role changes'.

Individual incentives

Individually determined plans are still by some way the most commonly employed incentive schemes in the UK, although they are heavily focused in sales and managerial areas. As you go about your daily life you will regularly encounter staff who are under their influence: in the shop where you buy your electrical goods, at your travel agent, amongst those charming young estate agents when you are buying or selling your home, or fixing up a mortgage or life cover, if you buy a new car, for those annoying people who ring you up on a Sunday afternoon with a 'wonderful opportunity' for double glazing or whatever; even your boss is likely to be in a management incentive plan. They are also evident in less obvious professions: for the electrician who rewires your house, the headmaster of your child's school, and for the inspectors assessing the standards of that school, for staff in the agency that issues your passport and the organisation that issues your National Savings certificates and Premium Bonds.

Thus if you go into a well-known central London department store, those ladies who greet you through a fog of perfume will be on targeted earnings of 50 per cent base pay and 50 per cent variable pay. The latter is made up of individual commission on revenue, that is a fixed cut of whatever they can sell to you. The schemes will be uncapped and the commission rate often increases beyond the targeted sales level, so the top sales people make considerably more than the average performer.

The manager of their department will have a more structured management plan, with a total incentive opportunity of 40 per cent of base pay, allocated across a number of key objectives, such as department total sales and costs versus budget, and in a third of cases also a measure of overall customer service levels. In Russian retailer 36.3, staff are on a 70:30 mix of fixed and variable pay, with the incentive dependent upon customer satisfaction as well as on sales results. For cabin attendants at low-cost airline Ryanair those proportions are reversed.

In the public sector, individual bonus schemes are generally much less aggressively geared, and they may also be much more closely tied to the performance appraisal and base pay adjustment process. Figure 4 shows the pay matrix that is used to adjust an individual's total pay at year-end in one government agency. As in a traditional base pay matrix, the fixed increase goes up with the performance rating, but as someone gets higher in their range and their pay more competitive, then the size of increase declines. Here, however, the total pay increase for high performers stays the same, it is just that the higher up the range you are then the more of this increase is delivered as a non-consolidated cash lump sum. A number of financial services companies have also successfully adopted this model.

Despite the arguments of the 'money doesn't motivate' school, the strongest researched difficulty with individual incentives appears to be that they have too strong an effect on individual behaviour and can encourage an excessive focus on the specific measures in the incentive plan, to the detriment of other important aspects of the work. One financial services company was forced

Figure 4 | Individual performance pay and bonuses in a government agency

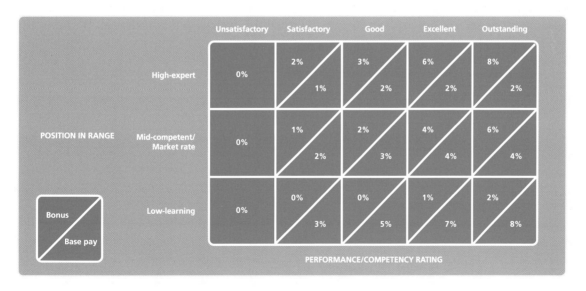

to dismiss two of its three highest commission-earning salespeople for mis-selling. Or to give another example, a manager told researchers from the University of Bath, 'we worship at the altar of team working, and then destroy it with our incentive plan'.

The incredible pressures and stress that high individual commissions can produce, to the detriment of customers and employees, are brilliantly described in David Dorsey's 'reality' profile of a year in the life of a regional sales force at Xerox, The Force. As the suicidal Willy Loman expressed it in Arthur Miller's play *Death of a Salesman* 50 years ago:

There used to be personality in selling, respect, comradeship and gratitude. Today it's all cut and dried, no friendship…so they take away my guarantee and put me on commission.

> **'…a well-balanced individual plan can support success by reinforcing business focus and culture change.'**

Yet there is an increasing body of evidence that a well-balanced individual plan can support success by reinforcing business focus and culture change. In a number of power utilities for example, structured objective-based bonus plans have been introduced for sales staff, who can range from those selling into industrial markets and who have never had any form of performance pay, to those acquired from agencies used to selling door-to-door on high sales commissions. A proportion of

the generally conservative and capped bonuses will be allocated to each of three to six personal objectives, which generally include a personal sales target, but often also cover quality and service measures, and specific goals such as building relationships with a key target client.

A team or overall business target is also commonly included, but this leads us into the rapidly growing field of combination plans.

Combination plans

Organisations are introducing combined approaches in one of two ways. Traditionally they have used a variety of different schemes to achieve different pay and business objectives. Thus the Coventry Building Society has a general corporate bonus for staff in support functions, where unit-based performance measurement is more difficult, as well as its branch sales bonuses. One of the road services organisations covers all of its staff with an annual corporate profit share. In addition, roadside service teams participate in more focused quarterly performance contests, with cash and non-cash prizes for the winning teams.

An increasing number of organisations, however, are attempting to combine these objectives of stronger individual incentive and collective reward within the same scheme, reflecting the real-life interaction of these variables on performance. Thus in a European furniture retailer, a bonus pool is created by the financial performance of the country operations. Payments to store staff, however, are modified by the quarterly performance of their own store in respect of four variables: sales, controllable costs, breakages and customer service ratings.

Thus using the matrix shown in Figure 5, assuming the country hit its profit target, then staff in a store who achieved an average of 110 per cent performance against the four targets would get a quarterly bonus equivalent to 4 per cent of their base pay. A store that failed to achieve its own 95 per cent of targets threshold would earn nothing.

These combined plans have often evolved out of simpler schemes. Thus over a third of insurance sales forces now have a team component within their commission plans. BP similarly introduced a combined all-asset performance goal into the rig-based gainsharing plans it had used in the North Sea.

The full line-of-sight from corporate through team to individual performance is also becoming evident in the design of plans, and approximately a quarter of new bonus and incentive plans in the USA have a corporate funding, a team and an individual component. A recently introduced example is in the commodities trading business of a large international group. For general staff in this business there is a 10 per cent annual bonus opportunity, with 5 per cent dependent on the margin performance of the business and 5 per cent on a series of function- and team-specific objectives. But payments are also modified up or down according to the individual performance assessment of staff. So while failure to achieve the operating margin threshold removes any chance of payment, so too an employee rated as unsatisfactory will receive no payment, whatever the performance level of the business and of their team. Direct trading staff have a higher bonus

Figure 5 | A French retailer's combination plan

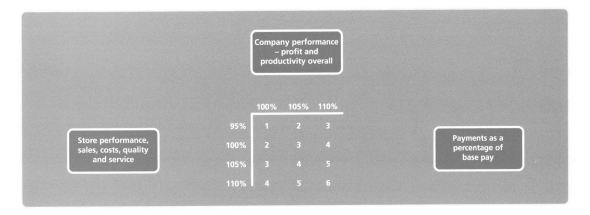

opportunity and a stronger weighting on personal performance, illustrating the flexibility of such schemes.

In fact, the majority of management incentive schemes below board level in UK companies are now of this mixed design. Typically there are components of business, divisional and personal performance in a manager's plan objectives, with the emphasis in weightings and payments shifting from the latter to the former measures as you move up the organisation.

Intellectually, these types of combination schemes are some of the cleverest and most interesting to design. The modelling can keep you busy for hours! They can also provide high variability in individual payments even within fairly tight overall cost constraints. Thus, a scheme generating, say, a 3 per cent of payroll pot based on corporate performance, might produce payments of 6 per cent to high-performing teams, and 12 per cent to high-performing individuals within those teams.

> '...while...these schemes on average get the highest ratings of effectiveness by the companies using them, they are also prominent in the ineffectiveness category.'

But while both the Towers Perrin and the ACA research show that these schemes on average get the highest ratings of effectiveness by the companies using them, they are also prominent in the ineffectiveness category. For although they potentially provide the best opportunities to educate employees about business performance

and combine both bonus /collective and individual/ incentive goals, (alleviating for example the problem of paying out high individual and team incentives in some areas when the organisation as a whole is performing badly), there are also a number of risks.

The prime one is over-complexity, with employees unable to understand all the different measures and their interactions, and therefore feeling that they have little impact on the outcomes and payments. Both the collective reward and individual incentive goals of such schemes can thereby be defeated. Experience shows that the most successful of them have evolved out of earlier distinct schemes, and they need a lot of effort and resources if they are to be introduced from scratch.

A corresponding advantage, however, is that the interrelationships can help to prevent a situation of distinct schemes in different parts of an organisation producing conflict and competition internally. They also help to avoid the situation, that was evident in a small and rapidly growing consultancy to the public sector. It uses aggressive individual executive and sales incentives to cover approximately 25 per cent of its people. But the other staff generally feel 'left out' and that their equally important efforts go unrecognised and unrewarded. In 40 per cent of cases these combined schemes cover all employees.

Another evident danger, particularly in these types of scheme, but across all types in view of the general trend towards balanced scorecard approaches, is what is known as the salami-slicing syndrome: using too many measures, each worth a small amount of the total payment opportunity and therefore not regarded as worth going for by participants.

Project and alternative bonus and incentives approaches

Just over a quarter of organisations in the Towers Perrin research were using bonus and incentive schemes that don't fit neatly into any of the categories already identified. Prominent amongst these are project bonuses, awarded usually on a one-off basis for the achievement of specific project goals. Thus, for example, National Lottery operator Camelot introduced a general staff bonus as part of its Project Rainbow to help retain the franchise when it recently came up for competitive tendering. This was designed to maintain staff morale, support the hard work involved in the re-bidding process and to help retain employees through a period of an uncertain future. The licence was successfully retained.

On a construction project, a scheme was developed to run throughout the three-year build period. An end-payment equivalent to one year's salary was made available to staff working throughout this period, dependent on overall completion to time and cost goals. The company faced severe cost penalties if the project overran. Annual progress and the payments so far 'earned' were regularly communicated to participants.

In addition, to enhance the incentive effect, the annual payment line up to completion was modified by a series of shorter-term key progress targets, such as tons of concrete laid in the early stages, or miles of cables installed later on. Achieving these targets each increased the end payment by up to 5–10 per cent. In the Towers Perrin research, 83 per cent of organisations using project bonuses rated their results as effective or very effective.

Figure 6 summarises some of the major characteristics of each of the types of plan reviewed in this chapter, and the situations in which they are most commonly found. But there is an increasing variety of creative, ad hoc and often frequently changing schemes evident amongst organisations in the UK. Ikea's recent granting of one Saturday's sales revenues as a bonus to share out amongst its staff is a well-publicised example.

The general 'loosening up' of bonus and incentive plan designs and the abandonment of the fixed, highly engineered, uniform and unchanging design model is evident in part of a government department. Here the HR function set out some criteria for the use of schemes. These included that they must be self-funding, team-based and publicised. Functions and branches then proposed their own schemes, which met these goals. The HR team at Abbey National has set out a similar set of criteria and more detailed design guidelines to help support its general strategic shift towards a greater use of variable pay. Many different locally tailored schemes now operate in different parts of

Figure 6 | Strengths and weaknesses of different bonus and incentive approaches

	1 Profit-sharing	2 Gainsharing
Main features	• Financial measures • Corporate level • All staff	• Operational measures • Unit level • Direct staff (typically 50–75% of total)
Strengths	• Ease of design/operation • Simple to understand • Rewards overall co-operation • Creates sense of corporate identity • No profit, no payout • Reinforces a primary business goal	• Provides direct incentive to employees to perform • Can incorporate wide range of measures of performance • Clear gains relative to cost of plan – self-funding on the site • Promotes co-operation on the site
Weaknesses	• No way of demonstrating impact on profits • Comes to be taken for granted • Influenced by factors outside of employees' control • No direct impact on employee behaviour	• Can be distant from individual employees • Can create friction between locations • Difficult to develop for indirect support staff • Susceptible to changes in business environment and organisation • Funding issue if company fails overall
Typical situations	• Very fast growth companies • Large intergated companies • Companies with strong relevant culture/ethos of stakeholding, etc • Legislative encouragement	• Decentralised industrial companies • Low interaction between units • Financial control management style • Wide scope for performance improvements

	3 Team schemes	4 Individual incentives
Main features	• Productivity, services, quality measures • Team level • Typically covers 10–25% of total staff	• Direct measures, eg sales • Individuals • Common for sales and management staff
Strengths	• Reinforce temwork • Provide strong team incentives within a team • Support other teamworking initiatives • Flexible to suit different teams in different areas	• Strong individual incentive provided • Differentiate on basis of performance • Make pay costs variable on an individual basis • Long history of use in many sectors • Align with individual performance management
Weaknesses	• Can encourage inter-team competition • Can raise funding issues if overall performance is poor • Problems if team structure is very fluid, and people are on a number of teams • Can demotivate high individual performers	• Can be a barrier to recruitment if base pay is too low • Can militate against teamwork • Can have damaging impact on measures not included in the plan
Typical situations	• Strong team ethic in the organisation • Team-focused measurement systems • Wide range of settings: financial services, oil, manufacturing, etc	• Decentralised/franchised operations • Aggressive individualistic cultures • Sales forces • Management populations • Particularly evident in fast-moving consumer goods, technology, financial services companies

Figure 6 continued | Strengths and weaknesses of different bonus and incentive approaches

	5 Combination plans	6 Project plans
Main features	• Wide variety of measures, often financial at top level and service and quality below • Typically 2–3 levels • Typically covers 50–75% of staff	• Specific project measures: time, budget, etc • Typically covering less than 5% of staff
Strengths	• Offer best of both worlds: incentive and reward • Reinforce co-operation across company and funding assured • Motivate through reference to local measures • Consistent but flexible approach	• Reinforce achievement of key project goals • Motivate project teams • Flexible design to suit specific characteristics of each project
Weaknesses	• Tend to be very complex to develop and operate • Employee understanding can be stretched • Danger of unexpected events affecting them • Can fail to achieve both incentive and general reward objectives	• What about people not working on a project? • Defining boundaries of who works on the project can be difficult • Need to be redesigned for each project
Typical situations	• Wide variety of situations • Probably prior experience of bonus plans	• Companies and industries organised on a project basis eg construction

the organisation, beneath the umbrella of a general profit-sharing arrangement.

Indeed, as illustrated in the public sector agency example above, as organisations seek to come up with new ways of addressing the intense cost, motivation and retention pressures they face in our competitive and rapidly changing economy, even the traditional barriers between fixed base pay and bonus schemes are breaking down.

Thus one retailer is siphoning off what would have been part of the base pay award over the next three years to help 'pump-prime' a store-based gainsharing plan, which will offer payment opportunities of up to 12 per cent to staff. Another retailer uses a fairly traditional merit matrix to distribute its base pay award to staff on

the basis of their individual performance. However, the size of the pay budget going into this matrix also varies according to the financial and sales performance of each outlet, so high-performing outlets get higher pay increases, but this budget is directed to the high individual performers at those locations.

> '...the traditional barriers between fixed base pay and bonus schemes are breaking down.'

Another business membership organisation also has a mixed base pay and bonus plan approach. If the organisation's revenue and cost budget is achieved then the negotiated base pay budget increase is implemented. If it is exceeded then a self-funded bonus scheme comes into operation.

But if it is not achieved then there are no bonus payments and base pay levels are frozen.

In the Consumer Group of pharmaceuticals giant Pfizer, managers who have moved beyond a certain point in their salary range do in fact put a proportion of their base pay at risk, in return for a significant annual bonus opportunity related to the achievement of key personal targets.

These examples also illustrate the importance of operating bonus and incentive schemes as part of a well thought through strategy of total rewards, in which the relative emphasis on the goals of, and interactions between, each of the various reward components is clear and agreed. Without such clarity the risks of failure with bonus and incentive plans are much higher. But just what is the general evidence as to the success or failure of these schemes, and what are the key issues that underpin their effective introduction and operation? This is the focus of the next chapter.

Case Study 1:
Abbey National – Bonuses as part of a performance, development and reward strategy

The Abbey National is one of the UK's major and fastest-growing banking institutions, with over 15 million retail customers, 29,000 employees and profits in 2000 of over £2 billion. Following a major review of its pay and reward policies, in 1998 it adopted a clear Performance, Development and Reward (PDR) strategy and it is within this context that the bank's approach to bonuses and incentives has evolved.

A key objective of PDR was to strengthen the relationships between performance and reward in the organisation. The uniform grade structure was replaced by a structure of job families and broad, market-related pay bands. Pay increases at the annual review now reflect an individual's performance in delivering on their job accountabilities and in achieving the accompanying performance indicators. With the general growth of variable pay in the financial services sector, bonuses and incentives are also playing an increasingly important role in cementing these relationships but, reflecting on the increasing diversification of their business, this is achieved in a multi-faceted and flexible way.

All employees are now eligible to receive a bonus of up to 5 per cent of base pay as a reward for group business performance, focused on the ratio of operating expenses to operating income. All are also eligible for a group-wide business performance bonus, which provides a common cash bonus opportunity of up to 8 per cent of base pay to staff, based on the level of group profits. This was initially operated as an approved PRP scheme.

In addition, share options are occasionally granted to all employees, to recognise special events such as the N&P merger and the acquisition of Scottish Provident.

These vehicles are designed, as the group's reward strategy defines it, to 'form an important part of the group's 'corporate glue', reinforcing the strong and distinctive Abbey National culture'. But, in addition, there are at least a dozen other incentive plans operating in different parts of the organisation, which reflect the specific character, functions and markets in which the bank operates. These have a more powerful incentive aim, targeted at specific individual or team goals.

Thus, in the retail bank, there is an individual area sales manager scheme, with annual payments based on the relative performance of managers. Corporate sales executives have shorter-term incentives based on exceeding personal targets. Reflecting the nature and organisation of the branches, the incentive for their staff is a points-driven combined scheme operating on a quarterly basis. Branch sales drive the value of points, and points depend on the specific activities of different roles in the branch. Meanwhile, in the treasury business a totally different set of arrangements operate, reflecting the specific characteristics of their market.

This tailored approach to incentives provides maximum flexibility, and helps to develop local understanding and ownership of schemes, but it is not a 'free-for-all'.

Schemes operate within a clear corporate framework of principles, established by the group HR function, and ensuring that schemes are congruent with the group reward strategy and with each other.

Group HR provides detailed guidance on introducing and operating schemes, to ensure that these core principles are adhered to in practice, and that problems that are common with such schemes are avoided. Scheme targets derive from divisional targets and payments are made only for above-target performance. A five-step process is set out, with clear approval points and criteria along the way.

Director of Group HR Development, Mike Cooke, and Reward Manager Rachel Baynes believe that this approach has to a large extent been successful in facilitating the growth of well-designed schemes in the organisation. However, as part of a wholesale review of the effectiveness of the PDR strategy, they are now considering a number of ways in which practices need to evolve. These are likely to take them in the direction of higher variable pay in specific areas, and with less emphasis on, and possibly some individual differentiation within, the business performance bonus.

- **Illustrates the research evidence on the success of bonus and incentive plans**

- **Specifies the four sets of factors that most strongly influence successful usage**

3 | Achieving effectiveness: strategy, structure, performance management and involvement

We have already considered individual case examples where bonus and incentive schemes have been associated with improvements in business performance, as well as some examples of inappropriate and damaging plans. In this chapter we consider the wider research on effectiveness and then draw out the four key issues that appear to be critical to the successful introduction and operation of all types of bonus and incentive: the overall rewards strategy that you adopt; the relationship to organisation and job design; the performance management processes; and, perhaps most critical of all, the context of employee communications and involvement.

The research record

The UK press coverage of failing merit pay schemes, and of executive bonus payments apparently unrelated to performance, tends to paint a fairly negative picture of the outcomes of bonus and incentive schemes. Yet in reality the research record is much more balanced, and in particular areas is far more positive.

Two sets of research studies are relevant in this regard. The first are individual case and meta-analyses of the effectiveness of particular plans. We have already referred to the performance gains associated with the use of bonus and incentive plans in a variety of organisations, ranging from power plants to steelworks to banks, call centres and department stores.

There are many other possible examples: the 46 per cent improvements in productivity associated with the use of gainsharing in British Energy's Scottish nuclear stations; the £1 million higher sales and 11 per cent lower staff turnover in those pubs owned by Whitbread Inns that piloted a cash bonus, compared to the remainder; the sales growth in Coventry Building Society's branches; and the improvements from 91 per cent to 99 per cent in service levels and 85 per cent to 91 per cent in quality measures in Eli Lily's Basingstoke plant.

Further afield, Simon Burgess describes some successful international examples, including:

◻ a 36 per cent growth in productivity and 9 per cent increase in average pay when Safelite replaced hourly wages with pay per item installed;

◻ and even a 75 per cent increase in fines per inspection levied by Brazilian tax collectors after the introduction of a bonus with team and individual components.

Meta-analyses suggest that these types of experience are not unusual. In respect of gainsharing for example, Bullock and Lawler's study of 33 companies found productivity gains ranging from 4.5 per cent to 24 per cent pa. The ACA's study of 2,200 collective bonus plans and incentive plans found an average performance gain generated for the company of over 200 per cent of the cost of the plan payments. Richard Freeman's recent research, presented at a CIPD rewards forum conference, found significantly higher sales and productivity growth amongst companies with profit-sharing and general employee share schemes.

> *'...HR managers...rated bonus and incentive plans as their most successful change initiatives...'*

Also at the macro level are a second set of studies demonstrating the associations between a 'basket' or 'bundle' of HR policies and practices, employee satisfaction, and business performance. Performance-related and variable pay schemes are always a component of this bundle: be it amongst the higher productivity companies in the Workplace Employee Relations study (averaging 17 per cent per employee); or those aerospace firms with significantly higher added value per employee than their competitors in Thompson's research; or those with higher shareholder returns in Pfeffer's study in the USA who displayed high pay with an incentive component.

Towers Perrin's study of 460 organisations in Europe found that those with the highest total shareholder returns use more incentive and bonus plans of all types, as well as more highly differentiated individual pay than the remainder. No wonder the HR managers in that research rated bonus and incentive plans as their most successful change initiatives, with many companies, including Dixons and the Coventry Building Society, also reporting a positive impact on the 'softer' goals of employee morale and teamwork, as well as the 'hard' financials.

The problems

Yet as Schuster and Zingheim express it, 'sometimes there is trouble in the variable pay paradise'. Research and case evidence also highlight the potential dangers and difficulties with the use of bonuses and incentive schemes.

Take the example of a UK roadside service organisation. The company had a marketing campaign promising to reach 95 per cent of stranded customers within one hour. It introduced associated quarterly team incentives for the agents receiving the emergency calls and dispatching the rescue patrols, based wholly on this key goal. For the first quarter all appeared to be going well, and the plan paid out. But then the difficulties emerged.

First, costs ballooned as agents made greater use of more expensive contactors to ensure the hour deadline was achieved. Second, once a vehicle had passed the hour point, those customers found themselves abandoned as agents diverted patrols to attend to those who could still be reached within the hour deadline. So much for those who say that financial incentives don't motivate!

Some of the commonest problems emerging from the research include:

◘ similar dysfunctional effects, generally resulting from an excessive focus on a single goal; to give another example, a management incentive plan in a glass company paid out to the senior team despite an 8 per cent drop in sales, because half of the payment was dependent on a separate cost measure, and costs had fallen even further; a great incentive to shrink the business! As Michael Armstrong puts it in his *Team Rewards* guide, 'the most measurable is not necessarily the most important'.

◘ deliberate 'gaming' by participants to maximise their payments for minimum effort

◘ controlling for the effects of factors outside of the control of the participants, which can produce windfall gains or a demotivating lack of payments for participants; a company recently removed a five-year management incentive plan which offered a very significant and uncapped bonus opportunity to participants for the achievement of a single fixed financial target; a simple and clear scheme undoubtedly, but the risks of it either being totally demotivating to participants or ruinously expensive for the company were simply too great

◘ the team/individual dilemma, of high individual performers feeling demotivated in collective schemes, but individual schemes having a detrimental effect on teamwork.

The real questions to address in this chapter are not therefore do incentive and bonus schemes work, but rather in what circumstances are they effective and how do I maximise their chances of success? Compensation commentators tend invariably to look at design features in explaining success or failure: keep the measures close to the people, keep it simple, introduce them in a business upturn, and so on. Yet while good design is obviously important, and this is considered in the next chapter, there appear to be four overriding determinants of success which, whatever your circumstance or scheme, you need to take account of.

Requirement 1: reward strategy

Successful bonus and incentive plans are not introduced as isolated pay initiatives but as part of a wider, integrated rewards and HR approach which addresses such fundamental questions as:

◘ what are the goals and success criteria for the scheme?

- how does it reinforce the success of the organisation?

- what is the emphasis on and role of the scheme relative to the other components of the reward package?

- how is the scheme supported by related HR initiatives?

Unless you can answer these questions then the evidence is clear that your scheme is likely to fail. Angela Bowey, for example, found that companies without strategic goals in the bonus measures and senior management support, and without related initiatives in training and communications, operated unsuccessful programmes. Schuster similarly found in the USA that successful gainsharing plans were introduced and operated 'with clear objectives, as part of a comprehensive management strategy to engage employees in a collective effort to achieve key business goals'.

Companies such as Cadbury and Dow, that have made a success of introducing value-based management, have used incentives to reinforce the concept. But as Haspeslagh illustrates, related activities in training, communication and organisation design were also vital.

James Welsh was at pains to point this out when he explained to the CIPD Rewards Forum the incentive reforms at Dixons. Improving customer service was not just about introducing a bonus scheme, but depended on a whole raft of initiatives: in management training, in technology and information available in stores, in better point of sale and after-sales support, and so on.

Requirement 2: structural fit

Alignment of your incentive plans with the structure of your organisation is a second fundamental requirement. Particularly with team incentive plans, there tends to be an assumption that 'a team is a team', when the term in reality covers many different types of co-operative (and sometimes not-so-co-operative) forms. An ad hoc project team, for example, will almost certainly require a different bonus, such as a project completion award, to a formally defined and fixed work team. Even amongst the latter, De Matteo found that employees rated team bonuses more highly if there was high interdependence between team members, and if they had prior experience of working in teams. Your plans have to be customised to support the specific activities and nature of each team.

Two structural variables are particularly important to consider in designing a bonus or incentive plan. The first is deciding on the 'vertical' level or levels in the structure of the organisation at which it will operate, be that organisation-wide, team- or unit-based, or individually driven. This obviously needs to relate to the goals of your scheme, such as providing collective reward and reinforcement, or a strong individual incentive.

It also needs to reflect the quality of performance information available at different levels in the organisation. You may want to reinforce customer service in your organisation with a powerful individual incentive. But unless you have the information to relate customer service measures back to individual employee actions then this will be impossible to deliver, and you may find that only a collective scheme will work.

You also need to ask yourself where, underneath vague value statements about teamwork and togetherness, is performance really leveraged and value added in your organisation? If, as a senior executive in a distribution company recently claimed, performance is really driven by a few key management employees, then a general profit share may well not be appropriate. But if there is genuinely a requirement for and culture of teamwork, then a team bonus will be more appropriate and will have more impact.

The second dynamic is the way in which people interact and co-operate 'horizontally' – between each other and in teams, and across units and functions. A business with highly differentiated and independent units is much more likely to have a wide variety of schemes tailored to the character of each unit. An accountancy firm, for example, with a corporate finance business will generally operate a different type and level of incentive scheme in that unit, reflecting practice in the market they operate in, compared to its general auditing and tax functions. Organisation-wide

rewards, meanwhile, can often help to reinforce the required co-operation and synergies in a more integrated structure and focused business.

At the level of the team, managers often fail to distinguish the importance of team working *within* teams relative to team working *between* teams. Situations with fixed and stand-alone teams are generally best suited to team incentives. If teams are fluid and dynamic and interact continuously then a fixed team incentive can be just as detrimental to co-operation and collective performance as an individual scheme.

Of course, few of our employers will not have initiated some form of reorganisation in the past year, and generally your bonus and incentive plans will need to evolve to reflect this if their success is to be sustained. As an example, a financial services call centre was initially organised into distinct service and product sales teams. Referrals between teams were vital, and so a centre-wide bonus scheme was initially used. However, changes in technology allowed them to introduce multi-skilled sales and service teams, which were preferred by customers. The bonus scheme was correspondingly changed to operate on an independent team basis.

> *'...an effective scheme needs appropriate, important and measurable performance targets, and effective communications and performance management.'*

Requirement 3: performance measurement and management

It seems incredibly obvious that an effective scheme needs appropriate, important and measurable performance targets, and effective communications and performance management. And yet this is so often where the intended benefits of a plan fall down in the reality of day-to-day life in the organisation. Plan measures may not link back to the organisation's strategic goals and add value to the business. Thus, in a telecoms company, a sales incentive delivering payments of 40 per cent of base salary to the telephone operators was based on individual sales. Yet the product was promoted with a massive TV campaign, all customer calls were 'inbound', the price was fixed, and the role was one of order taking not selling. Total sales would have been exactly the same without an incentive.

In other cases untested or unreliable performance measures have left incentive plans demotivating and ineffective. But often it is the broader processes of performance management, how targets are established and agreed, how performance is monitored and discussed, how payments are assessed and determined, rather than the specific measures used, that is critical to the success of any scheme.

In our ever more rapidly changing world it is getting more and more difficult to operate plans on a wholly formula-driven and quantitative basis. Enormous problems can arise with fixed formula schemes that fail to take account of future developments. Such as the case of the utility company that cut base pay levels for its industrial sales force and introduced a profit-based commission. Yet it failed to predict the average price of power contracts when setting the commission rates, and pay costs actually doubled with little return to the business.

But any degree of subjectivity in the operation of bonus plans depends on skilled managers with a strong and trusting relationship with their staff who are in the plan. It is scarcely surprising, then, that the highest performers in the Towers Perrin research, as well as making more extensive use of bonus and incentive plans, also gave the highest ratings to their line managers' skills in communications and performance management; or that alongside the wider use of bonus plans in Europe, over 80 per cent of organisations are taking steps to change and improve their performance management processes

The most successful incentive plans invariably operate as a seamless part of this wider performance management process, with the agreement of business and plan targets at the start of the period, ongoing communication, discussion and, if necessary, revision; and open review, assessment and payment determination at the end of the period. As the managing partner in one professional services firm has said, ' the bonus and appraisal systems need to be self-reinforcing if we are really to improve our results'.

Figure 7 | Building a value tree to determine job measures for an incentive plan in a major cable operator planning to open a new centre

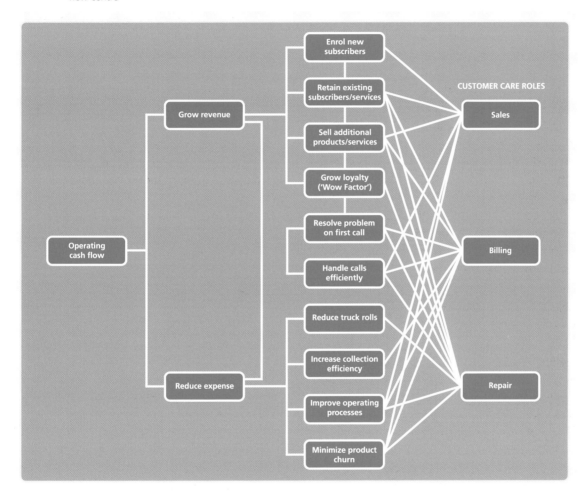

Another common problem is the use of business measures that employees cannot relate to or understand. Thus one car manufacturer introduced into its plants a new bonus plan with five measures, each related to one of its five corporate goals. Senior managers were delighted at the level of strategic alignment. Yet two-thirds of employees felt unable to affect these measures, and a majority favoured a return to their former productivity plan.

> *'...the more successful general staff plans were accompanied by consultation and involvement mechanisms and initiatives...'*

One solution to this need to link the top and bottom of the organisation, so to speak, in use at Towers Perrin is to build value trees. Figure 7 illustrates an example from one that was developed prior to introducing an incentive plan for the staff in a new facility of a major cable operator. Working with groups of employees, we broke down the key strategic goals of the business into their component parts, working down in the process to identify specific measures that the employees themselves could influence.

Thus an individual billing operator might initially feel able to do very little to help the company achieve its enormous cost budget. Yet the discussions identified many ways in which what they did contributed to the achievement of this target, for example by improving collection rates and reducing payment cycles. The incentive plan targets for each of the three main roles in the facility were then related to these identified

measures. Along with a range of other initiatives, they helped the new centre to exceed its sales target by 54 per cent in the first year, and to become the number one centre in respect of customer satisfaction levels.

Even in general profit-sharing plans, building the level of employee understanding of what drives profit, and how to grow it, are critical to plan success. Richard Freeman's research demonstrates that the more successful general staff plans were accompanied by consultation and involvement mechanisms and initiatives, rather than being introduced simply as a tax break and an accounting exercise. But this creation of a strong 'line of sight' also demonstrates perhaps the most critical ingredient of all in the success of any plan: employee communications and involvement.

Requirement 4: communications and involvement

When Michael Armstrong and I went back through the research on performance pay plans of all types some years ago, we found a remarkable level of consistency in the findings as to what explained the successful use of schemes. The correlation invariably was with the use of communications and involvement mechanisms and the understanding and support of staff. Some of the evidence is summarised in Figure 8.

Today, the growth of the knowledge and information economy and the increasing importance of human capital can only make this association stronger. As Jeffrey Immelt, the CEO of

GE puts it, 'the most important words in business today are "what do you think?" '. All of the studies listed in the first section of this chapter, without exception, demonstrate that employee involvement and consultation practices are, alongside bonus and incentive plans, critical ingredients in that performance-enhancing bundle of HR policies. Freeman, for example, demonstrates this tripartite relationship in his research, with those companies with profit-sharing and all-employee share plans, as well as experiencing higher productivity, also being much more likely to employ a range of employee involvement and consultation processes.

Figure 8 | Communications and process issues explain why incentives succeed in some situations and fail in others

Study	Factors correlating with success of incentives	Factors where no correlation is found
Bullock & Tubbs (1990) n=330	• Formal plan involvement structure • Staff involvement in plan design • Employee favourability • Participative management style • Controllability of targets* • Productivity rather than profit orientation* • Shorter payout periods*	• Size of organisation /plan membership • Union presence • Industry • Technology

Bowey & Thorpe (1982) n=63	• Extent of consultation
	  – involvement
	  – amount of communication
	• Supervisory skills/spans of control
	• Market/sales growth
	• Shorter payout periods*
	• Smaller size of membership*
		• Plan design in terms of:
		  – performance measures
		  – level of measures
		  – type of staff covered

Towers Perrin (1990) n=177	• Senior management commitment • Employee support/involvement • Emphasis on communications • Related HR activities, eg training • Performance measurement at levels below corporate • Shorter payout periods* • Operational or blended rather than wholly financial measures	• Organisation size • Union presence • Age of plan • Industry

* Weak correlation

Again, at one level this seems incredibly obvious. However well designed a bonus plan is on paper, if it is implemented, say, in a manufacturing plant where an employee who suggests a process change to improve performance against the plan goals is told to shut up and get on with his job, then it is not going to be a successful incentive plan, and probably not a successful company. Scanlon's original gainsharing proposals incorporated a detailed network of plant productivity committees, which were critical to the scheme's success.

Communications makes bonus and incentive schemes much more likely to be successful through a number of channels. Early consultation with staff, say through focus groups or an employee survey, builds employee understanding of why a scheme is being considered, and also develops trust and support in the resulting plan. It also adds immeasurably to the quality of the plan design, because nobody knows the potential to improve performance and the means of improving performance in a job better than the job holders themselves. People also like being involved and so you invariably get an element of the 'Hawthorne effect' in the process. Then, once the scheme is up and running, it is only through the actions, suggestions and efforts of staff that the targets in the scheme are actually going to be achieved.

'Employee consultation is one of the most important stages in developing a new or amended scheme...'

In the ACA incentives study, using task forces with employee representatives correlated strongly with the success of schemes and with improved staff perceptions of the link between personal performance and rewards. The case studies referred to throughout this guide, again virtually without exception, explain the critical importance of staff communications and involvement, and of adopting Lawler's definition of what a bonus scheme is.

As Martin Neville at Eli Lily puts it, 'nobody ever told me we over-communicated'. A whole variety of initiatives, including director briefings, business education sessions, and employee groups producing regular progress updates on the gainsharing plan, help to explain the success of their plan at Basingstoke, and the remarkable turnaround in plant performance.

Yet this message doesn't seem to be getting through to UK plc or department generally. Bonus and incentive plans may be expanding rapidly in UK organisations, but traditional habits of top-down management and pay secrecy appear to be hard to shift. According to the Industrial Society's latest report on bonus plans, 'the motivating effect of schemes is being undermined in many workplaces by employers' unwillingness to consult with their employees'. According to Will Hutton, 'designing schemes collaboratively with all stakeholders is a must if they are to have workers buy-in and any chance of success'.

Towers Perrin's research paints, if anything, an even bleaker picture, with only 7 per cent of organisations involving employees in plan design. Communications after implementation often receives a similar level of effort and attention, with only 29 per cent of companies feeling that their employees have a strong understanding of how their incentive schemes work, and a reliance on top-down, one-way channels. The 85 per cent looking for improved employee contribution to business performance, and using bonus plans to try to do so, can realise this aim only if they first give a much higher priority to the goals of building employee involvement and commitment. However, 79 per cent of the participants were planning increased investments in employee communications and related initiatives, such as line manager training in rewards management.

So when you assess the need for, or the effectiveness of, bonus and incentive plans in your own organisation, get your goals clear and business-aligned, structure the membership at the right level in the organisation, and use appropriate and tested performance measures. But don't forget the 'users' – the people on the receiving end of your wonderful scheme. Because if you do, frankly, you are wasting your time. If you are not prepared to talk openly and early with employees about the concept and design, then it is very unlikely that your scheme will be a success.

Employee consultation is one of the most important stages in developing a new or amended scheme, and it is this process that is outlined in the final chapter.

Case Study 2:
Establishing a framework for bonus and incentive schemes in a European software company

This software company, specialising in the development and sale of accounting systems, had grown very rapidly from its UK base during the later 1990s, and has now established sales operations in all of the major European economies, with in excess of 1,000 employees.

However, in keeping with many fast-growth entrepreneurial companies, the pay and incentive arrangements in this firm had grown up on a very ad hoc and individual basis. Cash bonuses and share schemes had essentially been negotiated in as part of the individual packages for mostly senior and a few key technical design staff, and they varied considerably in their nature and value. Hence they were supposed to be kept confidential, although their existence was well-known amongst the bulk of technical and support staff. Most countries did have a commission-type bonus scheme in place for all their direct sales staff, although again these did vary from country to country.

A review by the HR function highlighted a series of issues with this situation, notably:

• significant variations in the company's pay positioning against the external market on a base pay and total cash basis

• the inconsistencies and inequities in the current one-off schemes, which could not only produce unfairness between individuals, but also work against the implementation of a consistent strategy for multinational customers across Europe

- the lack of a strong financial recognition and reward for the bulk of staff.

The firm therefore developed a new policy and integrated framework for bonus and incentive plans across Europe. The objectives were to:

- enhance the motivation of staff to achieve and exceed business goals, with all staff having a variable pay component; this would also create a better balance between fixed and variable pay in the organisation's cost base

- better reflect market practice, to aid recruitment and retention

- operate schemes that are genuinely performance-driven and as simple and easily understood as possible

- be fully open in communicating schemes, to maximise the incentive effect

- recognise within a common framework the need for a variety of schemes, in order to:

  - enhance the incentive effect

  - recognise differences in roles and the nature of their contribution to business success

  - reflect variations in market practice

This last point was vital, for in an entrepreneurial culture the demotivating impression of imposing an inflexible uniform bonus scheme had to be avoided.

The framework of new schemes that was agreed and implemented is shown in Figure 9. There is now a management scheme operating across Europe, with the levels of bonus opportunity and emphasis on total European and local country performance varying according to the level of seniority of the role. Thus all country managers, for example, have a 25 per cent on-target annual bonus opportunity, based largely on their own country's sales performance.

The sales, pre-sales and professional services functions each have their own schemes, which mostly operate on a quarterly basis, with payments related to the achievement of individual performance targets. Sales staff are on a 50:50 base pay:variable pay mix at an on-target level, professional services consultants are on an 80:20 mix.

Finally, a new staff bonus scheme now covers all other employees in the company. The scheme is driven by the sales performance of each country, with sales revenue growth being the primary objective in this fast-growing enterprise, which still sees major growth opportunities. Quarterly sales targets are set and communicated, and progress against them is reviewed. At the end of the quarter, performance against targets is reviewed and payments are generated against a common sliding scale. Thus, for example, if the UK achieves only 75 per cent of target, then a payment of 2.25 per cent, equivalent to 9 per cent of base pay pa would be earned. If France achieved 120 per cent of its target, then the French employees would earn 4.5 per cent – a quarter of the maximum 18 per cent pa payment.

The quarterly timing was chosen to keep the scheme 'live' and a focus for business performance communications throughout the year, which can be a problem with annual profit-sharing type schemes. However, only two-thirds of the payment generated each quarter is actually paid out to staff. The remainder is banked and held over until the end of the financial year. This is designed to prevent the situation of early high payments being followed by poor performance and missing the overall sales target for the year. But to add interest at year end, the banked amount is subjected to a further modifier. If less than 80 per cent of the annual target is met then the payment is

forgone. At between 80 and 110 per cent of the country's annual sales target it is paid out in full. And if over 110 per cent of target is achieved then the banked amount is increased by 10 per cent.

The new arrangements have only been in place for less than a year, so it is too early to evaluate their success fully. However, the chief executive feels that there is now a much more united management team in Europe, and a much better business return on the cost of bonus payments. The common framework makes the mobility of management and sales staff between countries a lot easier for the HR function to effect, and the number of these moves is steadily increasing. And staff have generally reacted positively to having their obvious commitment to this friendly and fast-growing firm recognised with a financial bonus.

Figure 9 | European software company: the overall architecture of bonus schemes

- Sets out a process for developing appropriate plans

- Gives an overview and illustrations of the main work stages

4 | Developing schemes

Throughout this guide there has been an emphasis on the need to tailor the type, design and use of bonus and incentives plans to the specific goals, needs, character and circumstances of your own organisation. Resist those siren calls of 'off-the-shelf' and 'best practice' plans. But how do you do this? How do you make an assessment of this complex mix of variables as to whether these schemes are appropriate for you, and if so, what type or designs should be used?

This chapter sets out the main steps that you should take in making this type of assessment and shows how you can best go about introducing and operating the resulting scheme. For this process itself is a critical part of making a scheme successful.

The process

In planning a bonus and incentive scheme it is advisable to work through a seven-step process, as follows: an initial diagnosis and framing of the approach, then detailed design and preparation, followed by implementation, and ongoing review and modification.

The seven stages involved are illustrated in Figure 10. Although in reality the process is rarely as clear and sequential as this, nonetheless it provides a structure and an outline of the main areas you

need to cover. Each of these stages is briefly outlined in the rest of this chapter.

> *'Resist those siren calls of "off-the-shelf" and "best practice" plans.'*

1 Planning

This stage involves thinking through and agreeing how you are going to do the work, and who needs to be involved. Key components of the planning stage include:

◘ agreeing the goals and objectives of the work, addressing questions such as: are we looking at any type of scheme or the suitability of a particular type?; are we looking just at variable pay or at base pay and related communications and HR areas?

◘ Determining the scope of the work; it is also important to make responsibilities clear and avoid too much overlap and duplication

◘ specifying the detailed work stages, their logistics and timing, who needs to be involved, and who is responsible for which aspects of the work

◘ putting down any core principles, requirements or 'sacred cows' affecting the scope of the work; for example on one project some of the core principles that were developed at the outset included: no base pay reduction, strong economic proof, and everyone must participate

◻ developing the communications and involvement plan, which generally involves a brief early communication to staff that the work is underway, followed by regular progress updates; how staff can be involved and the role for any trade union representatives also needs to be established at this early stage

◻ clarifying decision-making responsibilities and the criteria for the ultimate decisions.

This last point is particularly important. A certain public sector body once commissioned a detailed set of proposed incentive plans. After some months' work these were presented to the board, who then declared that they disagreed with the whole principle of bonus payments funded by taxpayers' money!

Figure 10 | The seven step process

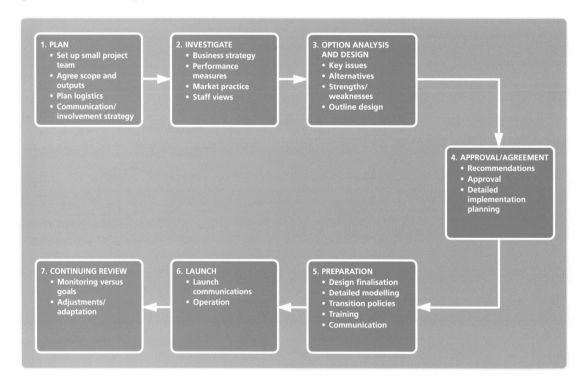

Typically, an organisation will form a small design group to do the detailed work on the project, and appoint some sort of policy or steering group to act as the decision-makers. For both groups it is important to agree, up front, the aims of the work and then to determine the basis on which decisions will be made. We all have our own personal views on bonuses and incentives, but the key is to get everyone agreed on the same set of judgement criteria, related to what is going to make the organisation successful in the future.

Thus when considering the appropriate plans to employ in the new European fuel ordering centre of a major oil company, six criteria were set out at the outset. On the basis of these, agreement could be reached as to whether, and how, to use such schemes. These criteria were:

◘ fit with the business goals

◘ alignment with the organisation and structure

◘ cultural alignment with the values and broader rewards 'deal' in the centre

◘ meeting the employees' expectations and needs, in this case reflecting those of a generally young and well-educated workforce

◘ competitive in the external marketplace

◘ appropriately positioned relative to rewards in the parent company.

This process also provides you with an agenda to go into the investigation phase of the work.

2 Investigation

This normally quite resource-intensive stage involves getting a full understanding of the current situation in the organisation, and its future requirements. It involves examining the organisation and the potential for bonus and incentives from three positions:

◘ from the business perspective, of what are the key goals and requirements in the organisation, and how the senior management believes they should best pursue them

◘ from the market perspective, of how competitors reward staff and use bonus and incentive schemes

◘ from the employees' perspective, as to how their needs and motivations can best be addressed.

Typical components in this stage include:

◘ senior management interviews and workshops; for example, with one professional services firm we had four two-hour meetings with the senior team agreeing the core principles and components of the rewards package and bonus schemes they need to employ, in the context of the organisation's business strategy and values; without this work, the three heads of very different business areas would never have collectively agreed with any single proposal that we subsequently presented to them

◘ industry analysis, to understand the performance dynamics of the sector and the sources of competitive advantage, as well as the strengths and weaknesses of the organisation relative to the competition, the sort of performance improvement opportunities and bonus scheme funding that might be available, etc; in one plant, for example, we found very high overtime and wastage levels, which gave significant scope for improvement and bonus scheme funding

◘ market analysis, to look at the levels of base pay and variable pay in the organisation relative to the external market; without necessarily copying what the competition is doing, it is nonetheless important to understand the context of typical practices and pay levels in organisations competing with you in product and labour markets; we also generally review the research and specific case experiences on bonus and incentive schemes in relevant organisations; for example, we organised visits by a financial services company to four organisations with a similar customer and values-focused culture, and they were able to look at, discuss and learn a lot from their experiences with their various plans

◘ a full analysis of current bonus, pay and performance management policies and practices in the organisation; what schemes are currently operating, what are their features, why were they introduced, how effective are they? how in reality do performance management processes, appraisal ratings and any existing bonus payments relate to each other? what other tools are available to recognise high-performing staff? how much differential in pay is there between high- and low-performing staff? is the performance appraisal process primarily developmental- or reward-oriented?

◘ consultation with employees, whether through staff focus groups or a broader employee survey, or both; surveys tend to indicate how strongly staff feel but generally discussion groups are a better forum to investigate why people feel the way they do, and what their likely responses to initiatives such as new bonus and incentive schemes might be; thus in the two plants of a pharmaceutical company in Ireland we found a relatively poor climate of industrial relations and staff suspicious of pay changes; but there was a strong sense of commitment to the success of the facilities and a perceived lack of recognition of employees' contribution to its success.

3 Issue identification, options analysis, and outline design

Pulling together all of this information, the project team would then:

◻ identify the key performance and motivation issues

◻ consider the general need for, and favourability of, the environment for introducing bonus and incentive schemes

◻ look at the pros and cons of the different types of scheme for the various groups of employees who could be covered by it

◻ agree the option(s) that best appear to address the identified goals, needs and issues.

Figure 11 | Example of a readiness assessment for the introduction of gainsharing in an Irish company

	Favourable	Unfavourable
Business/Financial	• Growing demand • Trend of performance improvements • Budgeted improvements • Major potential gains/returns	• Financial reporting and financial performance complexity • Raw material cost variations
Organisation/Operations	• Interdependence in manufacturing process • High wastage levels • Emphasis on product line organisation • Perceived influence of employees on performance/scope for improvement	• Corporate sourcing decisions • Importance of machinery • Future capital investment • Reorganisation of lines • Still central service sections • Lack of labour performance measures
Cultural	• Perception of 'good workforce' • General lack of recognition/reward • Desire to succeed • Under-utilisation of employees • Relaunching team briefing • Good employee/supervisor relationships	• History • Lack of internal communications • Lack of business understanding • Low involvement • Management style • Suspicion/mistrust/scepticism
Human Resources	• Stability in manning forecast	• Past redundancies
Pay	• Lack of incentive/motivation	• Tax situation

Thus, in the Irish pharmaceutical plants mentioned above, the issues that were identified were generally low performance levels relative to the competition, high fixed costs, and a lack of employee recognition and reward. For each aspect of our analysis we then looked at the pros and cons of the introduction of a scheme in the current situation, and this analysis is summarised in Figure 11.

The business potential, and related initiatives underway to really engage employees in the effort to improve, convinced us that a collective gainsharing scheme could play an important part in the plants' regeneration. This would have more meaning on the shop-floor than a profit share, while the quality of performance information and low trust environment made the use of any form of team or individual incentive out of the question.

> *'There are very few company situations in which there is a single, blindingly obvious solution to their pay, performance and motivation issues.'*

In a professional services firm, also with no existing scheme, the key issues were:

- a lack of variable pay relative to the competition, which was forcing them to adopt a very high market position on base pay

- the declining attractiveness of the firm to new recruits, which was increasing the importance of cash in their total rewards offering.

But rather than copying competitors with the use of a general profit-sharing scheme, the senior team favoured the option of more aggressive incentivisation for top performers, related to their personal and business unit goals.

In a privatised utility we found a number of potential reasons for using bonuses to help to instil a more commercial ethos and culture. This meant that we investigated a wide range of potential options. A profit share would suit the existing collective culture but fail to reinforce the stronger emphasis emerging on individual business unit and personal accountability. Team schemes would be very relevant in some areas, such as customer service centres, but inappropriate for, say, the sales force. The favoured option was a combination plan with overall firm funding, but with local variations in measures to suit the needs of each unit.

There are very few company situations in which there is a single, blindingly obvious solution to their pay, performance and motivation issues. Generally a variety of bonus and incentive alternatives and approaches, in conjunction with a range of other initiatives, have the potential to contribute to addressing these issues. All have their advantages and disadvantages in a given situation. The challenge is to select those that have the best balance of the two, with the greatest potential to move the organisation forward in a practical way.

4 Outline plan approval

It is essential to get approval for a particular approach and plan before doing the detailed design finalisation, testing and modelling. Otherwise you risk a significant investment of resources in something that then fails to get approved.

The process may involve a single presentation to the steering group or executive, or more commonly may involve a series of consultations and iterations with the key stakeholder groups. In a charity for example, we had a project team with some senior managers as well as line managers and employees on it, who worked up the outline proposals. Then the directors, followed by the trustees, negotiated and agreed its parameters and funding.

A useful framework in presenting the new or amended scheme would cover:

◘ the goals and rationale for the scheme

◘ the proposed membership

◘ the performance measures to be used

◘ the targeting methods

◘ the determination and levels of payment

◘ the timing of it

◘ brief administrative details.

Thus in our Irish example, we used this framework to discuss the key decisions and recommendations with the local executive.

The objectives of their plan were to:

◘ reinforce improvements in operational plant performance

◘ recognise the collective contribution of employees.

The membership was to encompass all employees bar senior management, who would be setting the targets. The plan measures were output, productivity, quality and service levels versus target in each plant. These would be measured and payment accrued on a quarterly basis, with regular reviews of targets, and adjustment in the event of unanticipated external circumstances.

In respect of payments, the scheme was to pay out 50 per cent of the value of the performance gains over target to staff, delivering between 0 and 25 per cent of pay to all staff on each site according to the level of performance achieved. Finally, in terms of administration, the scheme was operated on a non-contractual basis, to emphasise its variability. New starters during the year would participate immediately on a pro-rated basis, and there would be no payments for leavers.

As in this case, the outline scheme proposals are normally presented in the context of the issues we have identified and the other options that we have considered. This helps to explain why it is the best approach. The major benefits of the proposed plan and the outline costs and risks involved are also normally covered. This helps to ensure that expectations of the scheme are set appropriately, and that the requirements on senior management and everyone else to make it work are highlighted. Thus when we presented proposals to the senior partners in a professional services firm, we highlighted a number of areas to them, such as increasing attention and time devoted to performance management in their strongly client-oriented culture, in order for the scheme to be a success.

Some feedback to all staff, at least on major findings, would generally also be made at this stage before progressing.

5 Detailing and preparation

Components in this phase of the work would normally include:

☐ detailing all of the various design components – what level will the scheme be capped at, will there be thresholds, and so on?

☐ modelling and costing the scheme's operation under a range of different scenarios: expected, budgeted, historical, best and worst case, etc; this ensures that we fully understand the dynamics of the scheme, and that it can be both fully funded and provide reasonable payments to staff on the basis of possible levels of performance achievement

☐ depending on the nature and scale of the project, a pilot test of the scheme's operation, possibly in a part of the organisation, can often play an invaluable role in helping genuinely to assess its likely impact, and to tailor and fine-tune the subsequent roll-out and communications; typically, a favourable area of the organisation is chosen to pilot in, where the chances of success are very high, which can of itself build up a momentum behind the scheme, and set the informal 'grapevine' buzzing with more informed and positive rumours than would otherwise be the case

☐ defining operating, administration and control processes and responsibilities, specifying, for example, what will happen in the event of unexpected circumstances affecting the plan measures, who will be responsible for monitoring and communicating progress, and how we establish consistency and fairness in the targets that are set

☐ giving the scheme a name and identity that will have meaning to participants, preparing to communicate the scheme in advance of its launch, and then developing or linking in to the various communications and involvement vehicles to continue to feedback progress to staff, and obtain their input on a continuing basis thereafter.

Obviously, the issues that emerge in this phase vary hugely depending on the setting and the type of plan. There are a couple of common design issues, however, that regularly seem to come up. The first is in respect of the treatment of support functions and indirect employees, while the second is in regard to timescales.

Staff in support functions such as finance and HR tend to be treated in one of four ways:

◘ they have no incentive because their performance is more difficult to measure or their contribution is not seen to be direct enough

◘ increasingly however, organisations are developing performance metrics in these functions which allow them to have their own departmental plans, generally reflecting a mix of personal and departmental goals; however, payment opportunities may be lower than in direct operating units

◘ or support staff are aligned with performance in the departments that they serve; for example, the marketing staff in one company has an incentive driven largely by measures of sales performance

◘ or they are eligible for a corporate profit-share type of scheme, which is probably still the commonest approach in UK organisations.

Another common issue is the timing of payments. Behavioural research clearly demonstrates that we are motivated if we receive a reward as close as possible to the performance that earned it, which

encourages companies to use short incentive cycles. A number of management incentive plans have recently been moved from annual to more frequent performance and payment cycles. But the risks to the employer are that short-term performance is achieved and rewarded to the detriment of the longer term. The early period sees high performance and payments, but over the whole year performance falls back.

There is no set solution to this issue, and the appropriate balance needs to be established in your own setting and to meet your scheme goals. Some companies do attempt to balance the two by paying out a portion of scheme earnings on, say, a monthly basis, but retaining the remainder until the year end, to ensure that the overall performance remains sufficiently high to fund payments. But again, it needs to suit your circumstances.

6 and 7 Launch and ongoing operation

Most organisations probably do a pretty good job of communicating and introducing a new scheme. Enthusiasm is high, managers are briefed, glossy presentation material is produced and presented, and the scheme goes live. The problems typically come thereafter. The project team disbands, the momentum is lost and the scheme's profile, and often its impact, starts to wane.

Depressingly, fewer than a third of organisations in the Towers Perrin research made any attempt to assess the effectiveness of their scheme in achieving its original purpose. In many cases this was no longer clear to the participants or those now responsible for operating it.

'*...fewer than a third of organisations...made any attempt to assess the effectiveness of their scheme in achieving its original purpose.*'

Therefore, it is strongly advised at this stage to:

◘ make sure the responsibilities for operating and communicating the scheme on an ongoing basis are clear and followed through; in one company, for example, the members of the original design team became scheme 'champions' in their own area of the business, and other line managers were trained to act as coaches and facilitators for it

◘ bed down the scheme within as many as possible of the day-to-day operating processes in the business; ensure that the bonus goals, and progress towards them, are added to monthly management performance reports and briefings; make the scheme a regular agenda item in team briefings, trade union meetings and general staff communications; link the bonus to other recognition and involvement initiatives that may be under way

◘ conduct, on at least an annual basis, a formal audit of the scheme's operation and success; the Towers Perrin European research found that 20 per cent of organisations now have specific review criteria and/or audit groups in place, a marked increase over previous years.

The successful companies in the Towers Perrin study were not those that had run the same bonus or incentive plan for 20 years. Rather, they had a clear philosophy and goals for their schemes; they integrated them with their other business, performance and HR processes; and they made regular 'tweaks' and modifications to them, in order to reflect the changes in the organisation and its priorities, and to maintain interest and excitement in their operation.

Bonus and incentive plans are not magic bullets, and the time required to develop and operate them effectively should not be underestimated. But it is hoped that you have seen enough evidence in this short guide to convince you that it is worth the effort, with significant potential to leverage up both staff motivation and business results.

Case Study 3:
Lafarge Blue Circle – Paying through
partnership

Blue Circle is the largest cement company in the UK'
with approximately 1,600 employees based in the UK.
It was recently acquired by the French company,
Lafarge S.A, the global leader in the industry. The way
in which Blue Circle's pay and bonus arrangements
have evolved in recent years illustrates many of the key
points in this guide, most notably the importance of
high levels of staff communications and involvement.

History

Blue Circle made the headlines back in 1997 when it
signed the 'Way Ahead' agreement with its recognised
trade unions, a forerunner of the many partnership-
style agreements that are now evident across UK
industry

This was preceded by the introduction of annual hours/
integrated working throughout the UK in the mid- to
late 1980s, which was a pioneering move at that time.
The Way Ahead Agreement of 1997 enshrined an
employment security element linked to certain business
criteria, a long-term pay deal, total work flexibility,
harmonisation of terms and conditions between
manual and staff employees, and greater sharing of
business information with staff – in return for a joint
commitment to improving business performance. A
large number of projects have since been put in
motion, resulting in significant operational
improvements and productivity gains.

This approach appears to have fitted in very well with
the participative employee relations style of Lafarge,
and joint management/trade union teams from both
countries have been sharing experiences on a range of
issues at the European Works Council .

Meanwhile, a joint management, trade union and staff
sub-committee of the National Negotiating Forum
spent a year reviewing the company's approach to pay
including incentives/bonuses.

The review of pay

Traditionally the company paid its blue-collar staff a
fixed job rate, and white-collar staff within a range on
a merit pay progression basis. Various types of general
profit sharing had also been employed for all
employees, latterly on a tax-effective basis using the
Government's approved PRP scheme. Following the
'Way Ahead', pay progression was developed and then
introduced for works employees in 1999, related to the
acquisition of certified NVQs. In addition, a new
combination-level bonus scheme was implemented for
employees, related to the achievement of company-
wide and local targets. This was a discretionary scheme
requiring director approval. The local targets were
common to all sites and designed to give more local
impact to the scheme, with potential payments of up
to £1,200 pa.

A sub-committee was set up in 2001 to review the
NVQ-linked pay progression, in recognition of the fact
that this approach needed to change. The committee
members first established some key principles for pay

going forward, notably that pay and bonus schemes should be simple, fair, manageable and represent a 'win-win' opportunity for the company and employees.

The current arrangements displayed a number of shortfalls against these goals. Very few employees apart from new starters, and less than a fifth in total, had taken advantage of the certified skills pay system, despite the training opportunities and support provided. It was seen as over-complicated and too time consuming by the vast majority of experienced staff.

The bonus scheme, (which was separate from base pay) had had an undoubted effect in some areas, with national and local scheme safety measures successfully reinforcing a major improvement in lost-time accidents for example. But the scheme was still seen as remote by many employees, and with a general perception that targets were set at high levels and were difficult to achieve.

The sub-committee carried out internal reviews and looked at external market practice, before considering a range of change options. These included introducing merit pay for all staff (rejected on the grounds that there is little evidence of its effectiveness in a works environment), project bonuses, and recognition schemes.

The way forward on reward/incentives

The final details of the new pay approach have still to be negotiated, but there are likely to be three components: a three-year, inflation-linked general pay award; the use of a simplified skills pay system only for new works starters, and a separate modified discretionary bonus plan.

The architecture of the new gainsharing bonus that is planned is not radically different in its design from the previous scheme. There is likely to be a wider range of key performance indicators (KPIs) employed at both national and local level. Up to 50 per cent of the total bonus opportunity may be allocated across these targets at each level, with payments increasing up to a defined ceiling. But the significant difference is intended to be in the scheme's operating processes, with the objective of developing a much stronger degree of local input and impact. Bonuses will continue to be paid as a lump sum in the following year.

The national targets will be discussed and agreed in advance by the executive directors. And local joint committees will select the most appropriate performance indicators and agree targets from the broader menu of KPIs, including production, efficiency and safety measures. For example, five indicators could be selected in a works, with the menu including measures such as cost per tonne produced, plant running times, maintenance and contractor costs, mean time between stops, and sickness and accident rates, etc. The emphasis in setting targets will be on year-on-year improvement.

The idea of having a range of targets each with its own payment will assist in keeping interest in the scheme alive throughout the year. If it is linked to one target only, and there should be any early indication of potential failure, then the scheme could lose its impact.

According to the committee's report, the potential benefits of gainsharing are that it rewards team performance, empowers local teams and employees, and raises levels of interest in the potential to improve performance. Local Action Team members will be trained in understanding business plans and KPIs. They will play a key role in ongoing communications and discussions on the progress of the plan during the year, and how local targets can be achieved and exceeded.

According to National Employee Relations Manager, Mike Gibson, the perceptions were that previous schemes 'appeared to lack buy-in', and according to the committee's report 'there is no real confidence that the goals set are achievable'. But the greater degree of flexibility 'should give it a lot more local ownership', according to Gibson. 'We have local management/trade union teams – local action teams – who meet to discuss business and employee issues on a regular basis. Involvement in a scheme such as this can help focus the conversation on to the importance of company performance.'

Derek Warren, the national trade union steward for the AEEU and the Partnership Agreement Facilitator says 'Keeping things clear and simple is important. Most employees want the business to do well and if the goals are clearly defined we'll do our utmost to score them.'

Blue Circle's experiences have convinced them that the effectiveness of bonus schemes 'is not the money on its own, but the way it helps people to understand what we need to do, and how it keeps those KPIs up-front in people's minds: how they can save money, work more safely, or whatever. Provided that the performance versus targets is regularly communicated in an easily understandable format, using pictures and graphs, for example, then people, being competitive by nature are likely to respond in a positive way.'

Also under consideration is applying Lafarge's employee share scheme in the UK. This could be an additional performance reinforcement and employee involvement vehicle for them to use in the future.

Just as with their business improvement projects, Blue Circle's approach to pay is one of continuous review and improvement in a fiercely competitive and changing business environment. As the joint group defined them, with a focus on their three key aims of complementing business and employee needs, and ensuring arrangements are simple and non-bureaucratic, Blue Circle's high involvement approach is one that many companies looking for that elusive 'magic' bonus scheme design would do well to follow.

Bibliography

Abosch K, Reidy B. (1996)

'Supporting Teams through Reward Systems', *ACA Journal*, Winter.

Armstrong M. (2000)

Team Rewards. CIPD. London.

Atkins J. (2000)

Team-based Incentive Pay. Paper delivered at the Croners CCH conference on bonuses and incentives. London. 28 November.

Bowey A. (1983)

The Effect of Incentive Pay Systems. Department of Employment Research Paper, No 36. London.

Brown D.I, Armstrong M. (1999)

Paying for Contribution. Kogan Page. London.

Bullock R, Lawler E.E.III. (1984)

'Gainsharing: A Few Questions and Answers'. *Human Resource Management*, Vol 23, No 1.

Burgess S. (2001)

Incentives in Organisations: A Selective Review of the Evidence. Presentation at the University of Bristol CMPO. 26 April.

Confederation of British Industry. (2001)

Employment Trends Survey 2001: Measuring Flexibility in the Labour Market. CBI. London.

Culley M. (1998)

The 1998 Workplace Employee Relations Survey: First Findings. ESRC/ACAS/PSI. October.

De Matteo J.S. (1997)

'Factors Related to the Successful Implementation of Team-based Rewards'. *ACA Journal*. Winter.

Donkin R. (2001)

Blood, Sweat and Tears: The Evolution of Work. Texere. London.

Dorsey D. (1994)

The Force. Century. London.

Freeman R.B. (2001)

Improving Performance via Employee Ownership. Presentation to the CIPD Compensation Forum conference on the Future of Reward, 11 April.

Gross S.E, Duncan D. (1998)

'Gainsharing Spurs Record Productivity and Payouts at Amertisteel'. *Compensation and Benefits Review*. November/December.

Guest D, Conway N. (1998)

Fairness at Work and the Psychological Contract. IPD. London.

Haspelagh P, Noda T, Boulos F. (2001)

'Managing for Value: It's not Just About the Numbers'. *The Harvard Business Review*. July–August.

Hollinger P. (1999)

'Ikea to Give Staff World Takings for Day'. *The Financial Times*. 8 October.

Imberman W. (1996)

'New Auto Industry Standards Fuel Interest in Gainsharing'. *Compensation and Benefits Review*. September/October.

Incomes Data Services (2001)

'Portman Manages Performance'. *IDS Review*, No 246, August.

Incomes Data Services (2001)

'Bonus Schemes'. *IDS Studies*, No 705. March.

Industrial Relations Services (2000)

'Pay Prospects for 2001'. *IRS Pay and Benefits Bulletin*, No 507. November.

Industrial Relations Services (2000)

'Call Centres 2: Benchmarking Bonuses'. *IRS Pay and Benefits Bulletin*, No 506. October.

Industrial Society (2001)

Managing Best Practice – Bonus Payments. No 82.

Institute of Personnel and Development (1998)

Performance Pay Survey Summary. IPD. London.

Institute of Personnel and Development. (1994)

The IPD Guide on Team Rewards. IPD. London.

Katz D, Kahn R.L. (1964)

The Social Psychology of Organisations. Wiley. New York.

Keuch R.W. (2001)

'Pay for Performance is Alive and Well'. *WorldatWork Journal*, Vol 10 No 3. Third quarter.

Kohn A. (1993)

Punishment by Reward. Houghton Mifflin. Boston.

Lawler E.E.III. (2000)

Rewarding Excellence: Pay Strategies for the New Economy. Jossey-Bass. San Francisco.

Macadam J.L, Hawk E.J. (1995)

Capitalising on Human Assets: the Benchmarking Study. American Compensation Association. Scottsdale, Arizona.

Makinson J. (2000)

Incentives for Change. HM Treasury. January.

Milkovich K.T, Newman J.M. (1987)

Compensation. Business Publications. Illinois.

Miller A. (1986)

Death of a Salesman. Penguin. Harmondsworth.

Pendleton A, Brewster C. (2001)

'Portfolio Workforce'. *People Management*. 12 July.

Pfeffer J. (1998)

'Six Dangerous Myths about Pay'. *The Harvard Business Review*. May–June.

Pfeffer J. (1998)

The Human Equation. HBS Press. Boston.

Schuster J.R. (1987)

'Gainsharing: 'Do it Right First Time'. *Sloan Management Review*. Winter.

Thompson M. (1998)

'HR and the Bottom Line'. *People Management*. 16 April.

Towers Perrin. (1999)

Revolutionary, Realistic or Reticent? A European Study of Total Rewards. Available from the London office of Towers Perrin.

Voyle S. (2001)

'Glamour Boy to Advise Boots on Beauty'. *The Financial Times*. 18 September.

Wallace Bell D, Hanson C. (1989)

Profit Sharing and Profitability. Kogan Page. London.

Welsh J. (2000)

Using Competency-based Rewards to Provide Excellent Customer Service. Presentation to the CIPD Compensation Forum. London. 30 March.

West M, Patterson M, Lawthom R. (1997)

The Impact of People Management Practices on Business Performance. IPD. London.

Zingheim P.K, Schuster J.R. (2000)

Pay People Right: Breakthrough Reward Strategies to Create Great Companies. Jossey-Bass. San Francisco.

Also from the CIPD:

Directors' Pay in UK Plcs,
A CIPD Executive Briefing
Published 2000
ISBN 0 85292 893 9
£25.00/£12.50 (CIPD members)

Employee Share Ownership,
A CIPD Executive Briefing
Published 2001
ISBN 0 85292 902 1
£20.00/£10.00 (CIPD members)

Equal Pay Guide,
A CIPD Executive Briefing
Published 2001
ISBN 0 85292 920 X
£25.00/£12.50 (CIPD Members)

The Future of Reward,
A CIPD Executive Briefing
Published 2001
ISBN 0 85292 910 2
£25.00/£12.50 (CIPD members)

New Dimensions in Pay Management
by Michael Armstrong and Duncan Brown
Published 2001
ISBN 0 85292 883 1
£21.99/£19.79 (CIPD members)

Reward Determination in the UK,
A CIPD Research Report
Published 2001
ISBN 0 85292 907 2
£50.00/£15.00 (CIPD members)

Reward Strategies
by Duncan Brown
Published 2001
ISBN 0 85292 905 6
£25.00/£22.50 (CIPD members)

Stakeholder Pensions,
A CIPD Executive Briefing
Published 2000
ISBN 0 85292 890 4
£20.00/£10.00 (CIPD members)